RELAX KIDS
Little Book of Stars

52 Relaxation Stories
for Children under 5

RELAX KIDS
Little Book of Stars

52 Relaxation Stories
for Children under 5

Marneta Viegas

Illustrations by Nicola Wyldbore-Smith

**OUR STREET
BOOKS**

Winchester, UK
Washington, USA

JOHN HUNT PUBLISHING

First published by Our Street Books, 2014
Our Street Books is an imprint of John Hunt Publishing Ltd., Laurel House, Station Approach,
Alresford, Hants, SO24 9JH, UK
office@jhpbooks.com
www.johnhuntpublishing.com
www.ourstreet-books.com

For distributor details and how to order please visit the 'Ordering' section on our website.

Text copyright: Marneta Viegas 2013

ISBN: 978 1 78279 460 8

A CIP catalogue record for this book is available from the British Library.

Design: Stuart Davies
Illustrations: Nicola Wyldbore-Smith

UK: Printed and bound by CPI Group (UK) Ltd, Croydon, CR0 4YY
US: Printed and bound by Thomson-Shore, 7300 West Joy Road, Dexter, MI 48130

We operate a distinctive and ethical publishing philosophy in all
areas of our business, from our global network of authors to
production and worldwide distribution.

CONTENTS

www.relaxkids.com

Dedication

To Ronnie – my little bundle of magic. Thank you for sitting with me as I wrote and taking me on long walks to inspire new stories!

Foreword

Social stories are a wonderful way for children to explore learning and mindfulness. Children love to tell stories, role-play stories and teach others what they learn from stories. Marneta has captured the creativity at the heart of childhood with imagery and stories to guide mindful meditation in children. Research supports that mindful meditation calms the brain, inspires creativity and enhances cognitive and social-emotional skills.

Little Book of Stars is a gift of meditations children can do anytime, anywhere to get centered, experience peace and build a calmer inner life. With visual concepts such as the Magic Paint Brush, Superheroes and the Time Travel Machine, Marneta provides the words and actions needed to practice mindfulness as early as five years of age. The *Little Book of Stars* provides a beautiful and meaningful way for parents to connect with their children and for teachers to incorporate calming skills in the school day.

Marneta's Relax Kids creations build cognitive and social-emotional skills for all children but they have special meaning for children with anxiety, depression and anger as these children need actionable, accessible tools for self-regulation and mood management. Marneta has taken the guess-work out of helping your children develop calming skills with 52 meditations that are visually stunning and fun.

No other author is better suited to model for children, parents and teachers how to get calm and remain calm. As the author of over 20 books and relaxation CDs, Marneta is the princess of meditative calming for children. Her products are beautifully created, well-written and ready for immediate use, like a gift delivered to your door with a big red bow for learning and development.

Lynne Kenney, PsyD., Pediatric Psychologist, author, speaker
Author of *The Family Coach Method*

www.relaxkids.com

About the Author

Marneta Viegas set up Relax Kids in 2001. She had been running a successful children's entertainment business for thirteen years and noticed a change in children's behavior. Children seemed to be less able to sit still, listen and concentrate on her show. Using her degree in Performing Arts and techniques she had picked up from drama, singing and mime school combined with the meditation techniques she had learnt from a child, Marneta created a unique seven-step system for teaching children to relax. The classes were successful and Marneta now runs training for those who want to teach Relax Kids relaxation classes to children. Marneta has trained over a thousand people in her method from over 35 countries. Relax Kids is used in over half a million homes and schools worldwide.

If you would like more information about other Relax Kids products, relaxation classes and to train with Marneta, visit www.relaxkids.com

Marneta will be delighted to answer any emails marneta@relaxkids.com

Relax Kids products

Books

Aladdin's Magic Carpet
52 meditations using fairy stories (ages 3+)
The Wishing Star
52 meditations for children (ages 5+)
The Pants of Peace
52 meditations for children (ages 6+)
How to be Happy
52 activities and games for children (ages 5+)
Be Brilliant
Positive activities and cards for children (ages 5+)

CDs

Princesses
Superheroes
Up up and away
Nature
Relax and De-stress
Believe and Achieve
Little Stars (under 5s)
Self-esteem
Concentration
Anger Management
Anxiety and Worry

Cards

Star Cards – a treasure box of 52 cards to help children see and
develop their inner qualities
Mood Cards – 52 cards for positive moods

Download a FREE relaxation pack
www.relaxkids.com/freepack

How to use this book

For parents and teachers

These reflections incorporate simple relaxation exercises and visualizations designed to improve children's self-esteem and confidence and reduce stress and anxiety.

Practiced regularly, these exercises can have a profound effect on children's mental, emotional and physical wellbeing.

Set the scene by playing some soft music. You may decide to pick a random page, or take a page each day or week, moving chronologically through the book.

The affirmation at the end of each meditation is intended for the adult to use as a means of focusing attention and creating an atmosphere conducive to the children's concentration. We recommend you read this first.

After a moment's silence together, read the words slowly, with pauses, allowing the child to use his or her imagination.

You may like to read the words and then let the child drift into sleep, or you may discuss what they experienced, asking them to describe what they saw and how they felt. You may let them compare what they saw in their minds to the pictures.

Parents can read meditations to children at the beginning of the day, after school, in the evening or at bedtime.

Teachers can fit Relax Kids into any time of the school day. You don't need much room as children can listen to meditations sitting at their desk or cross-legged on the floor. Try reading a meditation at registration, during assembly, at lunch time, during circle time, after physical education, before going home or before an exam.

If you are interested in introducing relaxation to your child, why not send them to a Relax Kids activity class? Classes incorporate dance and movement, games, stretches, peer massage, breathing, positive affirmations and visualizations.

Relax Kids also runs a training program if you are interested in teaching relaxation skills to children.

relax kids

www.relaxkids.com

I am a...
Super Star

"I am a...

Beautiful Star★

Beautiful Star

I am a beautiful star.
I think about what makes me beautiful.

I have beautiful eyes that shine so bright.
I have a beautiful smile that makes people happy.
I have a beautiful heart that is kind and loving.

What makes you beautiful?

Close your eyes and stay nice and still.
Just pretend you are smelling a beautiful flower.
Hold the flower and take in a deep breath and smell the flower.

Can you smell it? Try that again.
Breathe in and smell the beautiful flower and breathe out
slowly.

Do you feel like a beautiful star?
Can you feel your beautiful face?
Can you feel your beautiful body?
Can you feel your beautiful heart?

Now stay as still as you can and think about being a smiling
star.
Who would you like to give your smile to?

Say out loud "I am a beautiful star, I am a beautiful star"
Now say it quietly "I am a beautiful star, I am a beautiful star"
Now whisper "I am a beautiful star, I am a beautiful star"

I am a...

Bright Star

Bright Star

I am a bright star.
I think about what makes me bright.
I have big bright eyes.
I have a bright smile.
I have a bright mind.

Close your eyes and take in a big breath and breathe out
slowly.
Try that again. Breathe in and breathe out slowly.

You are a bright star.
You shine like a star inside.
You are so bright.

Can you feel how bright you are?
You are bright inside and out.
You are a shining star.

Now stay as still as you can and think about being a bright
star.

Say out loud "I am a bright star, I am a bright star"
Now say it quietly "I am a bright star, I am a bright star"
Now whisper "I am a bright star, I am a bright star"

Brilliant Star

I am a brilliant star.
I think about what makes me brilliant.
I have a brilliant brain.
I have a brilliant head.
I have a brilliant life.

Close your eyes and take in a big breath and breathe out slowly.

Try that again. Breathe in and breathe out slowly.

You are a brilliant star.
Everything you think is brilliant.
Everything you say is brilliant.
Everything you do is brilliant.
Everyone thinks you are brilliant.

Can you feel how brilliant you are?
You are brilliant from the tips of your toes to the top of your head.
You are brilliant from your fingers all the way to your toes.

Now stay as still as you can and think about being a brilliant star.

Say out loud "I am a brilliant star, I am a brilliant star"
Now say it quietly "I am a brilliant star, I am a brilliant star"
Now whisper "I am a brilliant star, I am a brilliant star"

I am a...!

Brilliant Star

Calm Star

I am a calm star.
I think about things that make me feel calm.

I do things that make me calm.

I love sitting and listening...
and smiling and whispering...
and reading and relaxing.

What makes you calm?

Close your eyes and be nice and still.

Take in a big calm breath and blow out calm into the room.
Try that again. Breathe in calm and blow out calm.

How calm are your hands and arms?
How calm are your feet and legs?
How calm is your body?
How calm is your head?

Stay as still as you can and think about floating on a calm cloud.

Can you pretend you are lying on a soft calm cloud?
You feel so calm and quiet.

Can you feel your calm toes?
Can you feel your calm legs?
Can you feel your calm arms?
Can you feel your calm head?
Does it feel nice?

Take in a calm breath and blow all the way out.

Now say out loud "I am a calm star"
And now whisper "I am a calm star"
Now say it inside without talking "I am a calm star"

I am a:..

Carefree Star ⋆

Carefree Star

I am a carefree star.
I think about being a carefree star.
I am free from worries.
I am free of problems.
I am happy and free.

What makes you carefree?

Close your eyes and stay nice and still.
Take in a deep breath and blow all the way out.
Blow all your worries away.
Try that again. Breathe in and blow all your worries away.

You are a carefree star.
Your whole body is relaxed and free.
Your head is free from worry.
You are worry-free.
You are carefree.
You like being carefree and worry-free.

Now stay as still as you can and think about being a carefree star.

Say out loud "I am a carefree star, I am a carefree star"
Now say it quietly "I am a carefree star, I am a carefree star"
Now whisper "I am a carefree star, I am a carefree star"

Clever Star

I am a clever star.
I think about how clever I am.
I can paint and draw.
I can read and count.
I can sing and play.
I am very clever.

What makes you clever?

Close your eyes and stay nice and still. Think about how clever you are.

Take in a big breath and bring lots of air to your brain and blow out slowly.
Try that again. Take in a big breath and blow all the way out.

You are a clever star.
Your brain is very clever.
You can think with your clever brain.

Do you know how clever you are?
You are a clever star.
You think clever thoughts.
You speak clever words.
You remember clever things.

Now stay as still as you can and think about being a clever star.

Say out loud "I am a clever star, I am a clever star"
Now say it quietly "I am a clever star, I am a clever star"
Now whisper "I am a clever star, I am a clever star"

I am a...

Clever
Star ★

I am a...

Confident Star

Confident Star

I am a confident star.
I think about things that make me confident.

I stand tall like a confident tree.

I take big confident steps.
I have a big confident smile.
What makes you confident?

Close your eyes and be nice and still.

Take in a deep happy breath and blow out into the room.
Try that again. Breathe in and blow out.
Each time you breathe in and out you feel more and more confident.

Stay as still as you can and pretend you are looking into a mirror.
You can see how brave and confident and tall you are in the mirror.
You smile at yourself in the mirror.
Can you stand tall like a confident tree?
Can you take big confident steps?

Can you show your big confident smile?
How confident do you feel?
Does it feel great?

Take in a confident breath and blow all the way out.

Now say out loud "I am a confident star"
And now whisper "I am a confident star"
Now say it inside without talking "I am a confident star"

Co-operative Star

I am a co-operative star.
I think about things that make me co-operative.

I love helping others.
I love joining in.
I love waiting for my turn.
I love playing together.

What makes you co-operative?

Close your eyes and stay nice and still.
Take in a deep breath and pretend you are blowing on a feather.

Puff out and blow the feather.
Try that again. Take a deep breath and blow on the feather.

Are you a co-operative star?
Do you use your hands and arms to play nicely with your
friends?
Do you use them to help others?
Do you like being thoughtful?

Now stay as still as you can and think about being a
co-operative star.

Say out loud "I am a co-operative star, I am a co-operative star"
Now say it quietly "I am a co-operative star, I am a co-operative
star"
Now whisper "I am a co-operative star, I am a co-operative
star"

I am a...

Co-operative Star ★

Courageous Star

I am a courageous star.
I think about how courageous I am.
I am brave and strong inside.
I stand up for myself.
I believe in myself.

What makes you courageous?
Close your eyes and stay nice and still.
Take in a deep breath and breathe out hissing like a brave snake.

Try that again. Breathe in and breathe out hissing like a snake.

Can you feel how strong and courageous you are inside?
Can you feel how strong and courageous your heart is?
Can you feel how strong your bones are?
Can you feel how strong your head is?

Now stay as still as you can and think about being a
courageous star.

Say out loud "I am a courageous star, I am a courageous star"
Now say it quietly "I am a courageous star, I am a courageous
star"
Now whisper "I am a courageous star, I am a courageous star"

Creative Star

I am a creative star.
I think about all the creative things I can do.

I love drawing and painting...

and singing and dancing...
and playing and laughing.

Can you think of other creative things you can do?

Close your eyes and be nice and still.

Take in a deep breath and blow all the way out.
Try that again. Breathe in happiness and blow out happiness.

Imagine you are painting a happy picture.
What is in your happy picture?

Who is in your happy picture?

Can you colour in your happy picture with lots of bright
colours?

Stay as still as you can and think about your happy picture.
Can you see it?
How does it make you feel?
Do you feel proud and happy with your picture?

You are such a creative star!

Now say out loud "I am a creative star"
And now whisper "I am a creative star"
Now say it inside without talking "I am a creative star"

Keep your eyes closed and feel happy being a creative star.

I am a...
Dancing Star

Dancing Star

I am a dancing star.

I think about things that make me dance with joy.
Sunshine makes me dance with joy.
Fresh air makes me dance with joy.
Music makes me dance with joy.
Friendships make me dance with joy.

What makes you dance with joy?

Close your eyes and stay nice and still.
Take in a big breath and blow out bubbles of joy into the room.

Try that again. Breathe in and blow out bubbles of joy.
Can you see the bubbles dancing in the air?

You are a dancing star.
Can you feel the sunshine on your face?
Does it make you want to dance with joy?
Can you feel fresh air on your body?
Does it make you want to dance with joy?
Can you feel happy music?
Does it make you want to dance?

You are a joyful dancing star!

Say out loud "I am a dancing star, I am a dancing star"
Now say it quietly "I am a dancing star, I am a dancing star"
Now whisper "I am a dancing star, I am a dancing star"

Determined Star

I am a determined star.
I think about things that make me determined.
I am good at trying new things.
I keep doing something until I get it right.
I like doing my best.

What makes you a determined star?

Close your eyes and stay nice and still.
Take in a deep breath and now pretend you are blowing fire
into the room.
Try that again. Breathe in and blow out fire.

You are very determined.
Your whole body is strong and determined.
Your head is strong and determined.
Can you feel your determined body?
Can you feel your determined head?

Now stay as still as you can and think about being a determined
star.

Say out loud "I am a determined star, I am a determined star"
Now say it quietly "I am a determined star, I am a determined
star"
Now whisper "I am a determined star, I am a determined star"

I am a ....

Determined Star ⭐

Enthusiastic Star

I am an enthusiastic star.
I think about things that make me enthusiastic.
I enjoy doing new and exciting activities.
I enjoy meeting new friends.
I love learning new things.
I love having lots of energy.
I love life.

What makes you enthusiastic?

Close your eyes and stay nice and still.
Take in a deep breath and now pretend you are breathing in sunshine.
Fill your whole body with sunshine and blow it out slowly.
Try that again.
Take in a deep breath and breathe in sunshine and blow out sunshine.

How do you feel?
Are you an enthusiastic star?
Can you feel energy in your fingers and toes?
Can you feel joy in your head and your heart?

Now stay as still as you can and think about being an enthusiastic star.

Say out loud "I am an enthusiastic star, I am an enthusiastic star"
Now say it quietly "I am an enthusiastic star, I am an enthusiastic star"
Now whisper "I am an enthusiastic star, I am an enthusiastic star"

Fabulous Star

I am a fabulous star.
I think about things that make me fabulous.
I am friendly and fabulous.
I am fun and fabulous.
I am funny and fabulous.

What makes you fabulous?
Do you like being fabulous?

Close your eyes and take in a deep fabulous breath and blow
out.
Try that again. Take in a deep fabulous breath and blow all the
way out.

Breathing helps you feel fabulous.

You are a fabulous star.
Your body is fabulous.
You have fabulous legs and feet.
You have a fabulous back.
You have fabulous arms and hands.
You have a fabulous head.

Everything about you is fabulous.

Do you know how fabulous you are?
Do you like feeling fabulous?

Now stay as still as you can and think about being a fabulous
star.

Say out loud "I am a fabulous star, I am a fabulous star"

Now say it quietly "I am a fabulous star, I am a fabulous star"
Now whisper "I am a fabulous star, I am a fabulous star"

I am a...

Fantastic Star

Fantastic Star

I am a fantastic star.
I think about what makes me fantastic.
I am so bright and clever.
I am fun and friendly.
I am brilliant and special.

What makes you fantastic?

Close your eyes and stay nice and still.
Take in a big breath and as you breathe out say FANTASTIC.
Try that again. Take in a deep breath and blow out and say
FANTASTIC.

Your family think you are fantastic.
Your friends think you are fantastic.
Do you think you are fantastic?
Do you know you are fantastic?

Now stay as still as you can and think about being a fantastic
star.

Say out loud "I am a fantastic star, I am a fantastic star"
Now say it quietly "I am a fantastic star, I am a fantastic star"
Now whisper "I am a fantastic star, I am a fantastic star"

Forgiving Star

I am a forgiving star.
I think about how I can be forgiving.
I forgive others when they make mistakes.
I forgive others when they say 'sorry'.
I forgive others when they try their best.

I forgive myself when I make mistakes too.

Close your eyes and stay nice and still.
Take in a deep breath and breathe in lots of love.
Breathe out lots of love.
Try that again.
Breathe in lots of love and breathe out lots of love.

You are a forgiving star.
Your heart is full of love.
Can you feel how big your heart is?
It is full of loving thoughts and feelings.
You have a big heart.

Now stay as still as you can and think about being a forgiving star.

Say out loud "I am a forgiving star, I am a forgiving star"
Now say it quietly "I am a forgiving star, I am a forgiving star"
Now whisper "I am a forgiving star, I am a forgiving star"

Free Star

I am a free star.
I think about things that make me feel light and free.

I love skipping and jumping ...
and swinging on swings ...
and jumping in puddles.

What makes you feel light and free?

Close your eyes and be nice and still.

Take in a deep breath and blow all the way out. Breathe in and
blow out.

Stay as still as you can and pretend you are a balloon.
You are flying up into the air.
It feels so nice and light.
You feel so happy.

Can you feel your toes?
Can you feel your legs?
Can you feel your arms?
Can you feel your head?
Your whole body feels light and free.

Take in a deep breath and blow all the way out and feel yourself gently coming back to the ground.

Now say out loud "I am a free star"
And now whisper "I am a free star"
Now say it inside without talking "I am a free star"

Friendly Star

I am a friendly star.

I think about being a friendly star.
I like being friendly.
I make friends easily.
I am nice to others.

I share my things.
I laugh and smile with my friends.

What makes you friendly?

Close your eyes and stay nice and still.
Take in a deep breath and blow out love to all your family.
Try that again. Take in a deep breath and blow out love to all
your friends.

Does it feel good to be a friendly star?
Do you have friendly eyes?
Do you have a friendly face?
Do you have friendly arms?
Do you have a friendly heart?

Now stay as still as you can and think about being a friendly
star.

Say out loud "I am a friendly star, I am a friendly star"
Now say it quietly "I am a friendly star, I am a friendly star"
Now whisper "I am a friendly star, I am a friendly star"

Generous Star

I am a generous star.

I think about being generous.
I like giving gifts.

I like making things for others.
I like doing nice things for others.
I like helping out.
I like sharing.

What makes you generous?

Close your eyes and stay nice and still.
Take in a big breath and blow all the way out.
Try that again. Take in a deep breath and blow all the way out.

Do you like being generous?
Can you feel your generous heart?
Your generous heart likes giving and sharing.
Your generous heart likes thinking of others first.
Your generous heart likes being kind and selfless.
Can you feel your big generous heart?

Now stay as still as you can and think about being a generous star.

Say out loud "I am a generous star, I am a generous star"
Now say it quietly "I am a generous star, I am a generous star"
Now whisper "I am a generous star, I am a generous star"

I am a ... gentle Star

Gentle Star

I am a gentle star.
I think about things that make me gentle.
I am soft and careful.
I do things slowly and carefully.
I am quiet and gentle.
What makes you gentle?

Close your eyes and stay nice and still.
Take in a deep breath and blow gentle bubbles into the room.
Try that again. Take in a deep breath and blow out gentle
bubbles.

Does it feel good to be a gentle star?

Can you be gentle like a butterfly?
Can you feel your gentle fingers?
Can you feel how soft and gentle your hands can be?
Gentle hands are gentle to others.
Gentle hands are caring.

Now stay as still as you can and think about being a gentle star.

Say out loud "I am gentle star, I am a gentle star"
Now say it quietly "I am a gentle star, I am a gentle star"
Now whisper "I am a gentle star, I am a gentle star"

Good Star

I am a good star.
I think about being a good star.
I like being good.
It feels good to be good.
It feels good inside being a good star.
I like doing good things.
I like saying good words.
I like being good.

What makes you good?

Close your eyes and stay nice and still.
Take in a big breath and blow all the way out.
Try that again. Breathe in and breathe out.

You are a good star.

Can you wiggle your good hands?
Can you wiggle your good toes?
Can stretch your good arms?
Can you stretch your good legs?
And now stretch your whole body.

Now stay as still as you can and think about being a good star.

Say out loud "I am a good star, I am a good star"
Now say it quietly "I am a good star, I am a good star"
Now whisper "I am a good star, I am a good star"

Happy Star

I am a happy star.
I think about things that make me happy.
I do things that make me happy.
I love running and jumping...
and smiling and hugging...
and sharing and laughing.

What makes you happy?

Close your eyes and be nice and still.
Take in a deep happy breath and blow out happiness into the room.
Try that again. Breathe in happiness and blow out happiness.

Can you wiggle your happy toes?
Can you shake your happy legs?
Can you shake your happy arms?
Can you wiggle your happy fingers?
Can you nod your happy head?
That's right!
Stay as still as you can and think about the sunshine.
When everyone sees the sunshine they feel happy.
Sunshine helps us feel happy.
Can you pretend you are lying in the sunshine?
Feel the warm sunshine all over your body.
Can you feel your warm toes?
Can you feel your warm legs?
Can you feel your warm arms?
Can you feel your warm head?
It feels lovely.
Take in a happy breath and blow all the way out.

Now say out loud "I am a happy star"
And now whisper "I am a happy star"
Now say it inside without talking "I am a happy star"

Keep your eyes closed and feel warm and happy like a happy star.

I am a...

happy star ★

Healthy Star

I am a healthy star.
I think about things that make me healthy.
I love eating my fruit and vegetables and drinking water.
I love having fun, running and jumping and playing.

What makes you healthy?

Close your eyes and stay nice and still.
Take in a deep breath and now pretend you are blowing up a big balloon.
Puff out and blow up the balloon.
Try that again. Take in a deep breath and blow up the balloon.
Deep breaths help keep our bodies healthy.

Do you know how lucky you are to have a healthy body?
Can you feel your healthy body?
Can you feel your healthy head?
Can you feel your healthy legs?
Can you feel your healthy arms?

Now stay as still as you can and think about being a healthy star.

Say out loud "I am a healthy star, I am a healthy star"
Now say it quietly "I am a healthy star, I am a healthy star"
Now whisper "I am a healthy star, I am a healthy star"

Helpful Star

I am a helpful star.
I think about being helpful.
I like being helpful.
I like helping others.
I like being useful.
I enjoy making others happy by helping.

What helpful things do you do?

Close your eyes and stay nice and still.
Take in a deep breath and blow out slowly.
Try that again. Take in a deep breath and blow out slowly.

Are you a helpful star?
Can you feel your helpful hands?
What can you do with your helpful hands?
Can you feel your helpful arms?
What can you do with your helpful arms?
Can you feel your helpful head?
What can you do with your helpful head?

Now stay as still as you can and think about being a helpful
star.

Say out loud "I am a helpful star, I am a helpful star"
Now say it quietly "I am a helpful star, I am a helpful star"
Now whisper "I am a helpful star, I am a helpful star"

Honest Star

I am an honest star.
I think about things that make me honest.

I like telling the truth.
I like doing the right thing.
I like to own up to things I have done wrong.
I like to be honest.

What makes you honest?

Close your eyes and stay nice and still.
Take in a breath of clean fresh air and blow out slowly.
Try that again. Take in a breath of clean air and blow out.

Do you like being an honest star?

An honest star has a clean heart.
An honest star has a clear mind.
An honest star is happy.
An honest star likes telling the truth.
Everyone loves an honest star.

I am an...

Honest star ★

Now stay as still as you can and think about being an honest star.

Say out loud "I am an honest star, I am an honest star"
Now say it quietly "I am an honest star, I am an honest star"
Now whisper "I am an honest star, I am an honest star"

I am a...

Joyful Star

Joyful Star

I am a joyful star.
I think about things that make me feel joyful.

I do things that make me feel joyful.

I love skipping and jumping...
I love singing and dancing...
I love laughing and playing.

What makes you feel joyful?

Close your eyes and be nice and still.

Take in a lovely joyful breath and blow joy into the room.
Try that again. Breathe in joy and blow out joy.

Can you wiggle your joyful toes?
Can you shake your joyful legs?
Can you shake your joyful arms?
Can you wiggle your joyful fingers?
Can you nod your joyful head?
That's right!

Stay as still as you can and think about all the things that make
you happy and joyful. Can you feel that joy and happiness in
your heart?
Feel the joy all over your body.

Can you feel the joy in your toes?
Can you feel the joy in your legs?
Can you feel the joy in your arms?
Can you feel the joy in your head?
How does that feel now?

Take in a joyful breath and blow all the way out.

Now say out loud "I am a joyful star"
And now whisper "I am a joyful star"
Now say it inside without talking "I am a joyful star"

Kind Star

I am a kind star.

I think about things that make me kind.
I am kind to my family and friends.
I am kind to animals.
I am kind to plants and trees.

I like being a kind star.
It feels nice and warm inside.

What makes you kind?
Close your eyes and stay nice and still.
Take in a big breath and blow out kindness into the room.
Try that again. Breathe in and blow out kindness.

You are a kind star.
You think about others.
You are careful and thoughtful.
You have a kind heart.

Can you feel your kind heart beating?

Now stay as still as you can and feel your kind heart beating.

Say out loud "I am a kind star, I am a kind star"
Now say it quietly "I am a kind star, I am a kind star"
Now whisper "I am a kind star, I am a kind star"

I am a...

Laughing Star

Laughing Star

I am a laughing star.
I think about things that make me laugh.
I love funny stories.
I love funny people who do funny things.

What makes you laugh?

Close your eyes and stay nice and still.
Take in a deep breath and open your mouth and blow out a big
haaaaa.
Try that again. Breathe in and blow out with a big haaaaa.

Now take a deep breath in and blow out bubbles of happiness
into the room.
Watch the bubbles of happiness float in the air.
Breathe in and blow out bubbles of happiness into the air.

You feel happy.
Your whole body is laughing inside.
Can you feel your laughing fingers and toes?
Can you feel your laughing tummy?
Can you feel your laughing heart?

Lovely Star

I am a lovely star.
I think about things that make me lovely.
I am a good person.
I am nice and kind.
I am sweet and gentle.
I am loving.

What makes you lovely?
Close your eyes and stay nice and still.
Take in a deep breath and breath in lots of lovely feelings.
Now blow them out slowly.
Try that again.
Take in a deep breath and blow out lots of lovely feelings.

Do you know how lovely you are?
Can you feel how lovely you are inside?
Can you feel how lovely your body is?

You are lovely.

Now stay as still as you can and think about being a lovely star.

Say out loud "I am a lovely star, I am a lovely star"
Now say it quietly "I am a lovely star, I am a lovely star"
Now whisper "I am a lovely star, I am a lovely star"

I am a... Loving Star

Loving Star

I am a loving star.
I think about being a loving star.
I like being loving and giving hugs.
I like being nice and kind to others.
I like being a good friend.
I like being caring and loving.

What makes you a loving star?

Close your eyes and stay nice and still.
Take in a big breath and breathe out a big pink bubble.
Try that again.
Breathe in and breathe out a pink bubble of love into the room.

You are a loving star.

Can you feel your loving hands?
Can you feel your loving arms?
Can you feel your loving heart?
Can you feel your loving eyes?
You like being loving to those you know.

Now stay as still as you can and think about being a loving star.

Say out loud "I am a loving star, I am a loving star"
Now say it quietly "I am a loving star, I am a loving star"
Now whisper "I am a loving star, I am a loving star"

Lucky Star

I am a lucky star.

I think about how lucky I am.
I have a healthy body.
I have family and friends who love me.
I have a comfortable home.
I am lucky because I have everything I need.

What makes you lucky?

Close your eyes and stay nice and still and think about how
lucky you are.
Take in a deep breath and as you breathe out say 'thank you'.
Try that again. Take in a deep breath and say 'thank you' as you
breathe out.

You are a lucky star.
You are lucky to have a body that works so well.
You are lucky to have a brilliant brain.
You are lucky to have fresh air to breathe.
You are lucky to have fresh water to drink.
You are lucky to have good food.
You are lucky to be alive.
Do you know how lucky you are?

Now stay as still as you can and think about being a lucky star.

Say out loud "I am a lucky star, I am a lucky star"
Now say it quietly "I am a lucky star, I am a lucky star"
Now whisper "I am a lucky star, I am a lucky star"

Magic Star

I am a magic star.
I think about things that make me magic.

My body is magical, it does magical things.
My heart is magical, it pumps and keeps me alive.
My lungs are magical, they fill up with air so I can breathe.
My eyes are magical, they help me see.

I am a...

Magic
Star

What makes you magical?

Close your eyes and stay nice and still.
Take in a deep breath and now pretend you are blowing magic
dust into the air. Blow out all the magic dust.
Try that again. Take in a deep breath and blow out lots of magic
dust.

Do you know how magical you are?
Can you feel your magical body?
Can you feel your magical head?
Can you feel your magical brain?

Now stay as still as you can and think about being a magical
star.

Say out loud "I am a magic star, I am a magic star"
Now say it quietly "I am a magic star, I am a magic star"
Now whisper "I am a magic star, I am a magic star"

Patient Star

I am a patient star.
I think about things that make me patient.
I am good at waiting.
I am good at being still and quiet.

Close your eyes and stay nice and still.
Take in a deep breath and blow out as slowly as you possibly can.
Try that again. Breathe in and breathe out as slowly as you possibly can.

Think about how patient you are.
Are you good at waiting?
Are you good at slowing down like a snail?
Are you good at being still and quiet?

Can you make your fingers and toes stay patient and still?
Can you make your arms and legs stay patient and still?
Can you make your eyes and mouth stay patient and still?

Take in a big breath and breathe out slowly.

Now stay as still as you can and think about being a patient star.

Say out loud "I am a patient star, I am a patient star"
Now say it quietly "I am a patient star, I am a patient star"
Now whisper "I am a patient star, I am a patient star"

Peaceful Star

I am a peaceful star.

I have peaceful thoughts.
I whisper peaceful words.

I do peaceful actions.

What makes you feel peaceful?
What peaceful things do you like doing?

Close your eyes and be peaceful and still.

Take in a big peaceful breath and blow out peace into the room.
Try that again. Breathe in peace and blow out peace.

Can you blow peace onto your hands and arms?
Can you blow peace onto your feet and legs?
Can you blow peace into the air?

Stay as still as you can and think about being still like a peaceful
feather.
Can you pretend you are a soft peaceful feather?
You feel so peaceful and quiet.

Can you feel your peaceful toes?
Can you feel your peaceful legs?
Can you feel your peaceful arms?
Can you feel your peaceful head?
How does it feel?

Take in a peaceful breath and blow all the way out.

Now say out loud "I am a peaceful star"
And now whisper "I am a peaceful star"
Now say it inside without talking "I am a peaceful star"

Positive Star

I am a positive star.
I think about positive things.
I like thinking about sunshine and things that make me feel happy.
I like to create happy pictures in my head.
I like bright colourful things.

What makes you feel positive?

Close your eyes and stay nice and still and take in a deep breath.

As you breathe in, see if you can breathe in a rainbow.
And now breathe the rainbow out into the air.
Try that again.
Take in a deep breath and breathe in a rainbow and breathe out a rainbow.

You are a positive star.
You have lots of positive thoughts in your mind.
Positive thoughts are colourful and make you feel happy.
They are like rainbows.
Can you feel the rainbow in your head?
Can you feel the rainbow in your body?

Do you like being a positive star?

Now stay as still as you can and think about being a positive star.

Say out loud "I am a positive star, I am a positive star"
Now say it quietly "I am a positive star, I am a positive star"
Now whisper "I am a positive star, I am a positive star"

Quiet Star

I am a quiet star.

I like being as quiet as a mouse.
I like being as quiet as snow.
I can be as quiet as a cloud.

Can you be as quiet as a mouse?
Can you be as quiet as snow?
Can you be quiet like a cloud?

Close your eyes and be nice and quiet.

Take in a soft quiet breath and blow quietly into the room.
Try that again. Breathe in and blow out very slowly and quietly.

Can you make your hands and arms quiet?
Can you make your feet and legs quiet?
Can you make your whole body quiet?

Stay as still as you can and think about being quiet like a little mouse.
Can you pretend you are a tiny mouse in his little house?
Can you be still and quiet?

How does it feel being quiet like a mouse?

Take in a quiet breath and blow all the way out.

Now say out loud "I am a quiet star"
And now whisper "I am a quiet star"
Now say it inside without talking "I am a quiet star"

Relaxed Star

I am a relaxed star.
I think about things that make me feel relaxed.
I do things that make me feel relaxed.

I love squeezing and stretching.
I love lying down on soft cushions.
I love closing my eyes and resting.

What makes you feel relaxed?

Close your eyes and be nice and still.

Take in a big breath and blow out slowly into the room.
Try that again. Breathe in and blow out slowly.

Can you squeeze and stretch your hands and arms? And now relax.
Can you squeeze and stretch your feet and legs? And now relax.
Can you squeeze and stretch your whole body? And now relax.

Stay as still as you can and think about being floppy and relaxed.
Can you pretend you are a floppy puppet?
You feel so floppy and relaxed.

Can you feel your floppy toes?
Can you feel your floppy legs?
Can you feel your floppy arms?
Can you feel your floppy head?
How does your puppet body feel?

Take in a gentle breath and blow all the way out.

Now say out loud "I am a relaxed star"
And now whisper "I am a relaxed star"
Now say it inside without talking "I am a relaxed star"

Respectful Star

I am a respectful star.
I am well behaved.
I think about other people.
I am polite.

I always say "please" and "thank you".

I like being a respectful star.

Close your eyes and be nice and still.

Take in a big breath and blow out slowly into the room.
Try that again. Breathe in and blow out slowly.

Can you think about your hands?
Are they respectful?
Do they do nice things for others?
Can you think about your mouth?
Is it respectful?

Does it say kind words to others?

Stay as still as you can and think about being kind and
respectful.
You are a kind and respectful star.

Take in a soft breath and blow all the way out.

Now say out loud "I am a respectful star"
And now whisper "I am a respectful star"
Now say it inside without talking "I am a respectful star"

Responsible Star

I am a responsible star.
I think about things that make me responsible.
I look after my clothes and toys.
I help tidy up.
I look after pets and animals.
I am careful.

What makes you responsible?
Close your eyes and stay nice and still.
Take in a deep breath and blow out slowly.
Try that again.
Take in a deep breath and breathe out as slowly as you can.

Do you remember you are a responsible star?
You can use your hands to take care of things.
You are good at looking after your belongings.
You are careful.

Now stay as still as you can and think about being a
responsible star.

Say out loud "I am a responsible star, I am a responsible star"
Now say it quietly "I am a responsible star, I am a responsible
star"
Now whisper "I am a responsible star, I am a responsible star"

Safe Star

I am a safe star.
I think about things that make me feel safe.
I like feeling warm and secure.
I like snuggling up nice and cosy.

I like being under a soft fluffy blanket.

I love closing my eyes and feeling safe.

What makes you feel safe?
Where do you feel safe?

Close your eyes and be nice and still.

Take in a big breath and blow out slowly into the room.
Try that again. Breathe in and blow out slowly.

Stay as still as you can and pretend you are a tortoise nice and safe in your shell. You feel so warm and safe in your safe house.

Can you feel your warm toes?
Can you feel your warm legs?
Can you feel your warm arms?
Can you feel your warm head?
How do you feel?

Take in a gentle breath and blow warm air into your safe shell.

Now say out loud "I am a safe star"
And now whisper "I am a safe star"
Now say it inside without talking "I am a safe star"

Sharing Star

I am a sharing star.
I think about all the things I share with others.
I like sharing with others.
It makes me feel nice.

I like it when others share with me.

It makes me feel nice.

What do you like sharing?

Close your eyes and be nice and still.

Take in a big breath and blow bubbles of love into the room.
Try that again. Breathe in and blow out lots of bubbles of love.

Stay as still as you can and think about playing and sharing
with your friends.
Everyone is so happy.
Can you see everyone playing together nicely?
Can you hear everyone laughing?
Can you see everyone smiling?
How does it feel to see everyone happy?

Take in a gentle breath and blow all the way out.

Now say out loud "I am a sharing star"
And now whisper "I am a sharing star"
Now say it inside without talking "I am a sharing star"

Smiling Star

I am a smiling star.
I think about all the things that make me smile.
I smile at the sunshine and the rain.
I smile at my family and friends.
I enjoy smiling.
What makes you smile?

Close your eyes and stay nice and still.
Imagine you have a big smile in your tummy.
Now take in a deep breath and feel your tummy smiling.
Can you feel your tummy smiling? Now breathe out slowly.
Try that again.
Breathe all the way into your smiling tummy and breathe out
slowly.

Can you feel the smile all over your body?
Smiling makes our body feel happy.
Smiling is good for us.

Now stay as still as you can and think about being a smiling star.
Who would you like to give your smile to?

Say out loud "I am a smiling star, I am a smiling star"
Now say it quietly "I am a smiling star, I am a smiling star"
Now whisper "I am a smiling star, I am a smiling star"

I am a...

Smiling Star ★

I am a...

Special
Star ★

Special Star

I am a special star.
I think about things that make me special.
I am so special and unique.

There is no one else like me in the world.

I am one of a kind.
I am very special.
What makes you special?

Close your eyes and be nice and still.

Take in a big breath and blow out slowly into the room.
Try that again. Breathe in and blow out slowly.

Can you think about how special you are?
Can you remember all the special things you have done?
Can you think about all the special things in your life?
How does it feel to be so special?

Take in a gentle breath and blow all the way out.

Now say out loud "I am a special star"
And now whisper "I am a special star"
Now say it inside without talking "I am a special star"

I am a still star.
I think about things that make me feel still.
I am still when I am relaxing.
I am still when I am sleeping.
I am still when I stop and listen.

I like being still.
It is fun to be still.
I notice more things when I am still.

Close your eyes and take in a deep breath.
Hold it for a moment and blow out.
Try that again.
Take in a deep breath and hold and blow out again.

Did you feel still?

You are a still star.
Can you let your toes and legs become really still?
Can you let your hands and arms become really still?
Can you make your head become still?

You are very still.
It feels good to be still.

Now stay as still as you can and think about being a still star.

Say out loud "I am still star, I am a still star"
Now say it quietly "I am a still star, I am a still star"
Now whisper "I am a still star, I am a still star"

Strong Star

I am a strong star.
I think about things that make me strong inside.

I like being strong and brave.
I like being strong inside.
I feel good when I am strong.

I can be strong and calm inside.

What makes you strong?

Close your eyes and stay nice and still.
As you breathe in, you feel strong and secure.
Try that again.
Breathe in a big strong breath and breathe out slowly.

You are a strong star.
Do you know how strong you are inside?
Your body is very strong.
Your heart is very strong.
Your bones are very strong.

Can you stretch your fingers and toes and feel how strong they
are?
Can you squeeze your arms and legs and feel how strong they
are?
You are so lucky to have a strong body.

Now stay as still as you can and feel your strong body.

Say out loud "I am a strong star, I am a strong star"
Now say it quietly "I am a strong star, I am a strong star"
Now whisper "I am a strong star, I am a strong star"

Super Star

I am a super star.
I think about how super I am.
My body is super. It can run so fast.
My eyes are super. They can see into the distance.
My ears are super. They can hear tiny whispers.
My brain is super. It is the best computer in the world.

What makes you super?

Close your eyes and stay nice and still and think about how
super you are.
You are so super.
Take in a super breath and blow all the way out.
Try that again.
Take in a super breath and breathe out slowly.

Can you stretch your super fingers and arms?
Can you stretch your super legs and toes?
Can you stretch your super face?
And relax.

I am a...

Super Star ⭐

You are a super star with super star powers.
You think super thoughts.
You speak super words.
You do super things.

Now stay as still as you can and think about being a super star.

Say out loud "I am a super star, I am a super star"
Now say it quietly "I am a super star, I am a super star"
Now whisper "I am a super star, I am a super star"

Talented Star

I am a talented star.
I think about all my special skills and talents.
I can make things with my hands.

I can draw and paint and do crafts.

I can sing and dance and play sports.
What are you talented at?

Close your eyes and be nice and still.

Take in a big breath and breathe out slowly into the room.
Try that again. Breathe in and breathe out slowly.

Can you think about your talented hands and arms?
What can you do with them?
Can you think about your talented legs?
What can you do with them?
Can you think about your talented head?
What can you do with it?

Stay as still as you can and think about what a talented star you are!

Take in a soft breath and breathe out slowly.

Now say out loud "I am a talented star"
And now whisper "I am a talented star"
Now say it inside without talking "I am a talented star"

I am a...

talented star ★

Truthful Star

I am a truthful star.
I think about things that make me truthful.
I like to tell the truth.
I own up to my mistakes.
I say sorry when I make a mistake.
It feels good to be honest and truthful.

What makes you truthful?

Close your eyes and stay nice and still.
Take in a deep breath and now blow out slowly.
Try that again.
Take in a deep breath and blow out slowly.

Do you know how important it is to be truthful?

Can you feel your truthful mouth?
You mouth always speaks the truth.
Can you feel your truthful ears?
Your ears always like to hear the truth.

You like being a truthful star.

Now stay as still as you can and think about being a truthful
star.

Say out loud "I am a truthful star, I am a truthful star"
Now say it quietly "I am a truthful star, I am a truthful star"
Now whisper "I am a truthful star, I am a truthful star"

I am a...

unique Star★

Unique Star

I am a unique star.
I think about things that make me unique.
I am different from everyone else.
I love being different.
I am special.
I love being special.
What makes you unique?

Close your eyes and stay nice and still and take in a big breath
and blow all the way out.
Now think about all the things that make you unique and
different.
It is such a wonderful thing to be unique and special.

Your body is so unique.
There isn't another body like it in the world.
You are one of a kind.
Your face is so unique.
There isn't another face like it in the world.
Can you feel your unique face?

Now stay as still as you can and think about being a unique
star.

Say out loud "I am a unique star, I am a unique star"
Now say it quietly "I am a unique star, I am a unique star"
Now whisper "I am a unique star, I am a unique star"

Valuable Star

I am a valuable star.
I think about why I am so valuable.
I am so precious and valuable.

There is no one like me in the whole world.
I am so valuable.
I am a valuable star.

Close your eyes and be nice and still.
Take in a big breath and breathe out slowly into the room.
Try that again. Breathe in and breathe out slowly.

Your whole body is very valuable.
You need to look after it because it is so special.
You make sure that you eat well and get plenty of rest.
You drink water and exercise.

You look after your valuable body.
Can you give your whole body a big stretch? And let go and relax
Stay as still as you can and think about being like a valuable diamond.
Can you pretend you are shining like a diamond?

How does it feel to be so valuable?
Take in a gentle breath and blow all the way out.

Now say out loud "I am a valuable star"
And now whisper "I am a valuable star"
Now say it inside without talking "I am a valuable star"

Wise Star

I am a wise star.
I think about things that make me wise.
I am wise and smart.
I am a quick learner.
I am good at remembering things.

What makes you wise?

Close your eyes and stay nice and still.
Take in a deep breath and blow all the way out.
Try that again. Breathe in and blow it slowly.

Think about how wise you are.
You have a very wise head.
Your head is full of clever thoughts.
You are good at learning new things.
You are good at remembering.

Now stay as still as you can and think about being a wise star.

Say out loud "I am a wise star, I am a wise star"
Now say it quietly "I am a wise star, I am a wise star"
Now whisper "I am a wise star, I am a wise star"

I am a...

wonderful star ⭐

Wonderful Star

I am a wonderful star.
I think about everything that makes me wonderful.
My body is wonderful. It works so well for me.
My brain is wonderful. It is a wonderful computer.

What makes you wonderful?

Close your eyes, stay nice and still and think about how
wonderful your body is.
Every part of your body is wonderful.
Your eyes are wonderful because they can see.
Your ears are wonderful because they can hear.
Your nose is wonderful because it breathes in fresh air.

Take in a deep breath of wonderful fresh air through your nose
and breathe out as slowly as you can. Breathe in, breathe out.

Can you feel how wonderful it feels to breathe?
Can you feel how wonderful it feels to be alive?
Can you feel how wonderful it feels to be you?
Now stay as still as you can and think about being a wonderful
star.

Say out loud "I am a wonderful star, I am a wonderful star"
Now say it quietly "I am a wonderful star, I am a wonderful
star"
Now whisper "I am a wonderful star, I am a wonderful star"

OUR STREET
BOOKS

Our Street Books for children of all ages, deliver a potent mix of
fantastic, rip-roaring adventure and fantasy stories to excite the
imagination; spiritual fiction to help the mind and the heart
grow; humorous stories to make the funny bone grow; historical
tales to evolve interest; and all manner of subjects that stretch
imagination, grab attention, inform, inspire and keep the pages
turning. Our subjects include Non-fiction and Fiction, Fantasy
and Science Fiction, Religious, Spiritual, Historical, Adventure,
Social Issues, Humour, Folk Tales and more.

RELAX KIDS TITLES

Relax Kids: Aladdin's Magic Carpet

Let Snow White, the Wizard of Oz and other fairytale characters
show you and your child how to meditate and relax.

Marneta Viegas

Using well-known and loved fairy stories this is a gentle and
fun way of introducing children to the world of meditation and
relaxation. It is designed to counteract some of the tensions with
which we are all familiar at the end of a busy day, and offer
parent and children, from 3 upwards, together some quality
time to relax and share. The meditations and visualisations aim
to develop children's imagination and provide them with skills
that will be invaluable for the rest of their life. Using 52 fairy
stories and nursery rhymes like flying on Aladdin's magic
carpet, climbing Jack's beanstalk, flying through the air like
Peter Pan, swimming in the ocean with the Little Mermaid,
asking a question of the Wizard of Oz, listening to the sounds of
the forest with Snow White, and many others, children are
encouraged to go on magical journeys in the mind.
Hardcover: December 4, 2003 978-1-90381-666-0 $14.95 £9.99.
Paperback: November 28, 2014, ISBN: 978-1-78279-869-9,
$14.95 £9.99

Relax Kids: The Magic Box

Dip into a box of visualisation delights with these unique Relax
Kids meditations

Marneta Viegas

52 meditations for children (ages 5+)
The Magic Box is full of creative visualisations, meditations and
relaxations. Children can imagine they are on a tropical island,
flying into space, in a hot air balloon, time travelling and

leaving their worries on the worry tree. The book combines fantasy story meditations with deep relaxations, simple mindfulness exercises and positive affirmations. It is a great way to introduce meditation and mindfulness to young children.

Practiced regularly, these exercises can have a profound effect on children's mental, emotional and physical wellbeing.

Paperback: March 28, 2014 978-1-78279-187-4 $14.95 £9.99.

Relax Kids: The Wishing Star

Helping wishes and dreams come true with positive thinking, guided visualisations and affirmations for children

Marneta Viegas

Using guided meditations based around traditional stories this is a gentle and fun way of introducing older children to the world of meditation and relaxation. It is designed to counteract some of the tensions with which we are all familiar at the end of a busy day, and offer parent and children together some quality time to relax and share. The meditations and visualisations aim to develop children's imagination and provide them with skills that will be invaluable for the rest of their life.

For children aged 5 upwards.

Hardcover: January 20, 2005 978-1-90381-677-6 $14.95 £9.99. **Paperback:** November 28, 2014, ISBN: 978-1-78279-870-5, $14.95 £9.99.

Relax Kids: The Little Book of Stars

Helping children see their true star quality with simple visualisation exercises.

Marneta Viegas

The Little Book of Stars is the perfect way to introduce toddlers to relaxation and meditation. Each page explores a positive quality or value in an easy-to-understand and child friendly way. Examples include Happy Star, Calm Star, Brilliant Star and Generous Star. This book is designed to engage very young children while introducing them to simple relaxation and mindfulness techniques. Each relaxation exercise takes around 3-5 mins. The exercises in the book also aim help develop children's sense of awareness and self worth so promoting confidence and self-esteem. This book can be used at home, before nap time or bedtime or in nursery and kindergarten schools. Ages 2-5

Paperback: November 28, 2014, ISBN: 978-1-78279-460-8, **Price:** $ 14.95 £ 9.99

Relax Kids: How to be Happy

Teaching children the true meaning of happiness and helping them create happy family moments at home.
52 positive activities for children

Marneta Viegas

How to be Happy is a scrap book bursting with positive ideas, simple and economical activities and fun games. Each page includes colourful pictures and diagrams to explain the activity in simple child-like language. There are some in-book activities but this is mainly a book of ideas. This book is full of interesting ways to relax, have fun and be happy. It encourages spirituality for young children. Each chapter is a different activity such as how to make peace pebbles, how to make a chill out corner, how to be kind, how to relax, how to manage stress, how to write a personal prayer, how to make worry dolls. The book is written in child language and so would be easily accessible to young families. It makes it easy for families to embrace simple spirituality, acts of kindness and spiritual activities. The book is designed to bring families together and allow children to enjoy

spending quality time with their parents. It aims to help children manage their worries, anxiety and emotions whilst helping them grow up to be confident and happy.
Ages 4-7
Paperback: December 12, 2014, ISBN: 978-1-78279-162-1, $ 19.95 £ 9.99

Relax Kids: Pants of Peace
Allowing children to enter the world of their imagination with positive thinking and visualisations
52 meditation tools for children

Marneta Viegas
An innovative book that helps children get in touch with a wide range of inner qualities and values through creative meditation and affirmations exercises. Examples include shoe of confidence, cloak of protection, pen of appreciation and hat of happiness. Each meditation takes a positive quality or value and shows children in a creative and imaginative way how to develop that quality to improve their own life. This book encourages children to enjoy moments of calm and also helps develop their imaginations in a world of electronic gadgets. Pants of Peace is perfect for parents and teachers to read with children. The exercises are a toolkit to help develop children's mental health and well-being. Regular listening to these simple meditations can help children become more self-aware, positive and confident. This book can be used at home to help children relax or in the classroom. Ages 6+ The Relax Kids series is currently available in Europe and will be available in US from 2015.
Paperback: August 29, 2014, ISBN: 978-1-78279-199-7, $ 14.95 £ 9.99

CD available at http://www.relaxkids.com/UK/Audio CDs